GOD
CHOSE ME

DONNA MILLS

Fulton Books
Meadville, PA

Published by Fulton Books 2022

ISBN 979-8-88731-159-3 (paperback)
ISBN 979-8-88731-160-9 (digital)

Printed in the United States of America

Introduction

My name is Donna Marie Mills, and I am a Christian, a widow, and recovering alcoholic. I was born in a snowstorm, on February 8, 1960, in Chelsea, Massachusetts. My life has been stormy ever since. My story is not exciting or humorous; it's the story God chose me to tell. There is a lot of pain and trauma in my account, though it wasn't always bad. While I have not been to jail and have not found myself in an institution, that doesn't mean I always did everything I was supposed to; I never got caught. The other kids always called me goody two-shoes, but they were wrong. I am far from perfect, and I have made many bad decisions and gone down some pretty ugly roads. Yet somehow, God always found me and brought me back to Him for some reason.

I have always loved storms and winter, as it means I can curl up and read with a cup of hot tea or cocoa. I can often be found on my front porch during a thunderstorm in the summer, reading but mostly marveling at God's tremendous power. Although I am not partial to the wind, I love a good thunderstorm that rattles the walls and vibrates the windows. One of the most peaceful sights is watching snowfall; it's so quiet and gentle even in a blizzard.

God called me many years ago to write; I got my first diary when I was eleven; since then, I have written nearly every day for the better part of my life. Today, I journal twice a day and sometimes more. For me, writing is my way of talking to God. It's how I pray; it's how I communicate best. After my parents divorced, I stayed in contact with two of my cousins and a grandmother through letters. Yep, that's right, snail mail, a practice I continued until I divorced the first time. I still write letters on occasion. Writing helps me calm down the squirrels in my head that threaten to drive me crazy, those thoughts that won't stop no matter what I do. Something I should have said, or not, something I should have done differently. The list of ways I can beat myself up mentally goes on and on, and I know I am not alone.

I got my first computer in early recovery and mentioned that I considered writing a book. My friend thought it was a good idea, yet I felt insecure and talked myself out. My thinking was, *Maybe someday*. The truth is, I never felt that my story would be interesting enough for anyone to want to read. But then twenty-five years later, God put it in my heart to write my story for the newest edition of *The Big Book*, Alcoholics Anonymous. At first, I was still hesitant until I went through my regular daily routine. Finally, the urge to write was so intense I could not ignore it any longer. I get up before anyone else, read a meditation book, listen to guided meditation, and then write on an average day. Whether my story gets published or not is not the point; the point was that I was inspired and guided by God, and I obeyed.

I chose to ignore that call all those years ago, yet I have heard I was a writer on multiple occasions. So, as I sit here listening to the birds sing, it's a lovely spring morning, and the sun is shining. Although it's not quite warm yet, it is comfortable. I love being outside when I write when the weather permits. I love the smell of fresh air and feeling the breeze on my skin. If it's not warm enough to be outside, I will sit in front of a window to admire God's handiwork. The glorious colors of the sunset, the clouds slowly drifting across the sky. I will do my best to tell you the many ways God blessed me even when I did not believe.

In reading these words, I hope that you don't wait as long as I did to learn how to live a God-led life; I am still learning. I won't tell you how to live for God; we each have our journey, though I encourage you to find yours. I am a compassionate person; I will cry over the minor little thing, TV commercials, love stories, random acts of kindness, or a compelling sermon; it got me in a lot of trouble early on until I learned to accept who I am. This story is about one hard-headed tenderhearted woman's journey back to God who couldn't see what was right before her, even when she had heard. I finally decided to listen after twenty-five years. I ask that as you read, remember I am not a victim; God was with me every step of the way, even when I did not know or believe it.

The Journey Begins

Most people rarely remember anything that happened to them during the first five years of their lives, and there are some things I wish I could forget. However, I know now that God needed me to remember all the things that shaped my life and made me the woman I am today. Who that is, I am still learning. I don't know how my parents met; they divorced before I was old enough to ask. My dad was in the Navy, and my mom was just out of high school. They were only six months apart in age. They were married in November 1959.

My earliest memory is walking across my grandfather's house room into my grandfather's arms one bright day. I was near the living room doorway, and the sun was shining through the plate glass window. My grandfather was sitting in his recliner next to the window. It was a huge picture window, and the sun shining through was very bright. He leaned forward in his chair and told me to come to him. My mother says I was six or seven months old; I've always been in a hurry, though I don't know why. I remember jumping on my aunt while she was asleep and my grandfather telling me not to wake her as "she is a bear if you wake her up." I thought it was fun. My aunt was around twelve at the time. My grandfather was not a very tall man, and he had a way of telling a story that made even the silliest stories seem believable.

One of my favorites was the story of how the mercury lights came on. One night, we were sitting on the back porch as the lights were coming on, and he asked if I knew how they came on. I did not. He said, "There is a little man who lives in the lights. When he lights the lamp, the spark of that light sends him through the wire to the next one." He had a story for everything, and I wish I could remember them all. Grandpa was from Newfoundland and spoke with an accent, so listening to him tell his tales was fascinating for me.

The first time I flew in an airplane, I was almost two years old, and my sister was a few months old. We were moving to Rothbury, Michigan. I don't remember much about that trip except that I got to sit by the window. The journey to Michigan started a lifetime of running for me, not the kind of running that wins awards, the type of running that keeps a person in isolation and fear. As you will see, my running took me to some pretty sordid places, and while some were beautiful, I was running from myself and God.

I remember November 22, 1963; it was snowing, I was three, and tragedy struck our nation in a big way. Yet that is not why I remember it; here is what I remember. My mom was distraught, and we went across the street to the neighbor's house. The grownups were gathered around the television in the kitchen, crying and talking. There were probably six or seven children in the house. It was absolute chaos. Being oblivious to what was happening in the kitchen, we played and ran up and down the basement stairs. Suddenly my sister missed a step and fell headfirst down to the concrete floor; everyone froze. The next thing I remember is my grandmother was there. We were standing in the driveway waiting to cross the street when she said the words I would carry with me for the next twenty-five years, "This was your fault." The snow falling felt like cold tears. I bowed my head and went with my mom to our house and my room while they took my sister to the hospital. I was ashamed, even though I did not know what that meant. We would not know the extent of the damage that colossal goose egg on her forehead would cause until several years later.

Sometimes my parents and I would watch TV shows like Lawrence Welk, Hee Haw, and Westerns. Then I would *dance* and be silly during the musical shows because it made my parents laugh. I loved music and loved to dance and sing. Music has always played an enormous part in my life; there are times when a song can bring tears to my eyes and break my heart, and other times a piece will fill me with so much joy I feel my heart will burst. But I have no rhythm, so dancing was not something I pursued though I was a pretty good singer. I was in the choir from sixth grade until tenth grade. Then my dad said it would not help me in my life and was, therefore, unnecessary. Later I was in church choirs until I was about five years sober.

We were not far from Lake Michigan, so many of our storms came over the lake. I remember one in which the wind was so strong the trees were bending over nearly in half. I couldn't understand how they could bend like that without breaking. I was in awe. We did not go to church then, so I did not know about God yet.

The Quiet Phase

I started kindergarten when I was five, and my cousin, who is nine days younger than me, was in the same class. I loved it, so many people and so much to learn. I still love learning new things and am always thrilled when I find willing teachers. I try to remember that a bad example can also be a good teacher; pain is a great motivator.

Our kindergarten and first grade were in an old one-room schoolhouse in those days. I thought it was beautiful, the hardwood floors and the chalkboards that covered the whole wall. The room felt fun and busy. The kindergarten class was full of color, with letters, numbers, and vibrant shades tacked to the walls. The first-grade room was much more somber; one wall had a chalkboard from one end of the room to the other. The walls were dark paneling and made the room feel warm and inviting. Then in second grade, we moved to the new building. I am one of those kids that it seems like the harder I try to be good, the more trouble seems to find me. So in second grade, I went to the principal's office for the first time. I always sat in front of my cousin because my name came before hers alphabetically. One day she passed me a note. I didn't want to get in trouble, so I gave it back to her; I got caught.

About a month into the school year, I came home from school. It was half a day back then, and my mom had fixed me a peanut butter and jelly sandwich. As I sat at the table eating, I looked out the kitchen window and saw a thin stream of smoke. There was a factory next door, and it was on fire. I said, "Mommy, look." She called the fire department, and my sister and I stood and watched as the fire department worked diligently to put it out. The smoke was now thick and black. We could smell it; it burned our eyes, yet we could not look away. We could feel the heat from roughly fifty yards away. Finally, the fire got so hot that the concrete blocks were starting to melt, and the fireman said we might have to evacuate.

My sister and I are a year apart in age, and most of the time, we got along pretty well; we would play outside together, build forts with our blankets on our bunk beds, and raid the garden for carrots and radishes. I would tie knots in the blankets to the top bunk and drape them down over the bottom bunk, and we would play with our toys in the near dark. My dad would plant a garden every year. I am not a big fan of vegetables, but there is nothing like a carrot or a fresh radish. We would rinse them off with the hose until they caught. We still got them out of the garden, and we learned to clean them off on our clothes.

One thing I loved and still miss to this day is the whippoorwill's song. My dad and I would sit in the backyard in the evening and listen as the sun went down. Sometimes my sister and I would play in the woods behind our house. Unfortunately, there was a pile of broken glass near the woods, and one day I fell and cut my hand. As my mom said, I was in shock, or it didn't hurt. I never cried. I simply walked into the house and showed her my hand. I believe that was the second time I had to get stitches; I don't remember the first time, though I do have the scar. The sight of blood didn't bother me then.

Some days we would play in the basement while mom did laundry; we had a wringer washer that I thought was very cool. I loved watching mom do the laundry using that machine. The big tub had two rollers on top, and once the clothes got washed in the tub, she would run each piece between the rollers. Then she put it all back in the tub to rinse, then back through the rollers to the clothesline. When she did laundry, we would play hide and seek or dress up in my dad's Navy hats.

Sometimes mom and dad would go out for dinner or something and leave my sister and me with a sitter. We always knew when they were going out because that was the only time mom bought potato chips and soda. My sister and I managed to get our hands on these forbidden snacks, and we hid in our bedroom closet, eating them until we got caught. When you have two little girls under five, and they get quiet, you look for them.

My dad had a sweet tooth, and mom would buy him these butterscotch candies and hide them in the highest kitchen cabinet. I loved them also, and once in a while, I would climb onto the counter and get some. Somehow I never got caught. I adored my dad; he was my first superhero. I was a *Daddy's girl.* I would follow him everywhere. My favorite was watching him shave; I don't know why, and it must have driven him crazy. Mind you, this was before disposable razors. I would watch as he got the brush wet and put the shaving cream on his face. Then I would giggle at the funny faces he made when he shaved. Strange kid, yeah, I know.

I would define life as pretty average; Dad worked the second shift, and Mom stayed home with us. At least nothing of significance happened except for the birth of my brother, David, in 1965, until September 1966. I was six, in the first grade; I had come in from school. I got off the school bus and saw my brother playing in front of the house. It was a picture-perfect fall day, and the sun was shining; the leaves were falling. The air was a little crisp, and I was anticipating my favorite TV show. My dad was asleep and did not usually wake up until time to get ready for work. My mom and sister were taking a nap. Mom woke up for a few minutes when I turned on the TV and asked where David was. I told her he was outside. She went to the back door and told him to come in and get a cookie. Then she lay back down on the couch, leaving the cookie on the table for him, and went back to sleep. While I sat watching the *Mickey Mouse Club*, someone knocked on the door; when I opened the door, a man held my brother David in his arms.

There was blood all over his shirt, and I remember being scared. Today the sight of blood sends me into a state of delayed panic; I do what I can to fix it, then I go to a quiet place and fall apart. Later, I heard I was hysterical. Then again, my grandmother came and said those exact words, "This was your fault." So another tragedy lay at my feet, and I carried it. Again I retreated to my room; I didn't even watch the *Mickey Mouse Club* again for a long time.

I continued to go to school and play with my siblings and cousins, yet somehow I got it that I had to be perfect. Don't get me wrong; I still did things bad and got in trouble, although I did my best to be good when it mattered. And by all appearances, I was an average child who happened to be good in school, and I enjoyed reading. Reading became my escape. I would open a book and disappear from the world around me. I don't have a great imagination, but I could visualize the words on the page into pictures in my head.

During the two years after David's accident, we stayed at the house in Rothbury. We sometimes would visit my aunt and uncle and their four kids. We would see family on the weekends, or they would come to our house. Sometimes we would go to my grandparent's house and play our favorite games.

My aunt and uncle lived on a farm, so there was plenty of space for us to run. When we got together with our cousins, we played hide-and-seek. We played in orchards, climbed trees, and played games like king of the mountain in the hayloft. I loved the orchard's deep, dark earth, plowed and dusty. The smell of freshly tilled soil, fresh-cut hay, and manure reminds me of simpler times. We were daring each other to do ridiculous things like eating rabbit food. Sometimes the grownups would go out to dinner, and my oldest cousin watched us all. When we didn't do what we were supposed to do, she would threaten to hit us with her hairbrush. That hairbrush became infamous for a long time.

Then in February 1968, my brother, Michael, was born. I stayed with my aunt and uncle until my mom returned from the hospital. One morning my aunt woke us up to show us a rainbow. I had never seen one before and thought it was breathtaking. Whenever I see a rainbow now, I remember that it is a promise from God, and I remember that first one.

After that, we moved to a farmhouse in Shelby, Michigan, between the second and third grades in the summer. I loved that old house; it had an attic full of treasure that my sister and I would explore, even though it was forbidden. Fortunately the house sat at the end of a dead-end road. There was a church with a cemetery across the street.

I had never seen a ghost or a scary movie, so living across from a graveyard was astonishing and peaceful. There was a silence in that place that I could feel. It touched me and made me feel very calm inside. After that, I would not go into the cemetery as it felt intimidating to me. Instead, I would spend hours exploring the orchards and fields around the house. Shortly before school started, I went to the orchard to read; I climbed into a pear tree and stepped into a yellowjacket's nest. I don't know how many times I was stung. I remember I couldn't see, and it was hard to breathe; Dad took me to the doctor, and I got a shot. I was supposed to get injections once a week, but my dad said it was too expensive and too much trouble. So after that, I stayed out of the orchard.

A few months later, in November 1968, my dad came and picked me up from school and took us to the airport. My parents were getting a divorce. I don't know why but I was agitated; I did not want to leave my dad. So my mother, siblings, and I moved back to Revere, Massachusetts, with my maternal grandparents.

I do not understand why my parents divorced. I asked them both when I was older, and I got two different answers. We had visited my grandparents a few times, but I didn't know them. They lived in a big yellow house on a bustling highway, so we were only allowed to play in the backyard. They bought us a swing set, and there were Adirondack chairs all around the yard. Eventually, we were allowed to explore the neighborhood and found a park where I could take the other kids, and I could read.

It didn't take long for me to figure out that I would have to follow a new set of rules, and my mom checked out. At first, she would get us up and ready for school, though in a short time, it fell on me to get us up and prepared for school. My grandmother was a seamstress, so she made clothes for my sister and me to wear to school and church. We were Catholic, so the church became a big part of my life; I would go to catechism, confession, and mass. At Christmas, we would go to Midnight Mass, and I loved it when I was able to stay up late enough to go. I loved going to church, although I did not understand very much about God back then. All I knew was that if I were good, I would get to go to heaven, and misbehaving was a sin that would get me sent to hell. So every Saturday, I would go to confession and perform the penance the priest assigned.

I was about to learn a lesson that I found difficult to comprehend and more challenging to unlearn. Secrets, keeping them, holding on to them, never letting them see the light of day for fear of bringing shame, guilt, and disgrace to the family; this was how I grew up. First, I wasn't allowed to talk about my parent's divorce or anything in our house, good or bad. Then when I was about ten, my uncle was in a motorcycle accident. When I saw him in the hospital, I was terrified because he looked like a mummy. Later, I talked to a friend in the yard, and my grandfather heard me; I was grounded for a week because I had told someone outside the house what had happened.

After that, I got so good at keeping secrets that I lived in a fantasy world for a while. A world created by the many books I read. Until I got my first diary at eleven, I kept everything bottled up inside me. Writing became an outlet for me to express my feelings and a way for me to talk about all the things I couldn't share or comprehend.

Like most children of divorce, I thought it was my fault, and if I were a better kid, my dad would come and get us and take us home. So before I got my diary, and because I had a hard time making friends, I often walked and talked aloud to myself, figuring out how to cope with my life. Today I realize I was praying.

Before third grade, I changed schools four times; I was a child of divorce, I had two disabled siblings, all my clothes were handmade, and we were on welfare. Making friends became difficult, and books became my best friends. It's difficult to make friends when you aren't allowed to talk about anything, and trust was something of which I had very little. I loved school and learning, so making friends didn't seem that important, and I knew getting good grades was essential to keep my mom happy. Also going to school was a way for me to escape whatever was going on at home at the time. My favorite subjects were history and English, no surprise there. The field trips we got to go on were incredible, the old North Church, Bunker Hill Monument, and the U.S.S. Constitution "Old Ironsides," to name a few. The Old North Church, with its stained glass windows and the sun shining through, was simply stunning. The family boxes were stunning with their red cushions and white high-backed benches.

I climbed to the top of the Bunker Hill monument and was astounded by the sight of how everything looked so small. The cold, damp, spiral staircase seemed to take forever to climb, and the top windows were tiny. Nevertheless, the view was well worth the climb.

And Old Ironsides was amazing; seeing and hearing how the sailors lived was impressive. Also the wood was so shiny and clean; it looked brand-new even though she is two hundred twenty-five years old. Whenever I visit the Constitution, I do it primarily because I love hearing the stories of how they lived and what their lives were like while aboard a ship.

I truly loved our public library; it was a stately old brick building in the adult section with hardwood floors upstairs. The children's area was downstairs and a lot more colorful and bright. Somehow I thought I could not get in trouble if I read, so I spent hours reading everything in the library. I especially liked mysteries; I read all the Nancy Drew and Hardy Boys books, then discovered magic and things like King Arthur. When I was reading, I would get lost in the story, sometimes imagining that it was real and my life was a story. Next I found comic books and superheroes, superpowers, and a whole new world opened up for me in my early teens. The library at school was tiny and limited, so I got permission to go to the public library. At ten years old, I had to take a city bus to get there, and I came home with four or five books each week.

I eventually ventured out of the house, going to the park and the beach, where I met girls in the neighborhood. During the next three years, I hung out with friends and went to the beach, the park, and the library. Sometimes, we would go ice skating at the local arena or the movie theater on the weekends. I took Michael to see the original *Willie Wonka and the Chocolate Factory* in 1971. There were times when I would go to the theater alone to watch a movie, although it was more the find a quiet place to sit in the dark. I enjoyed the deep, soul-seeking peace of sitting in the dark, a practice that has followed me most of my life. I find nothing more peaceful than sitting in a dark room and letting my mind wander wherever it wants, not thinking, just being.

I was learning to run; whenever things got difficult at home, I would go somewhere else, the beach, the park, anywhere that wasn't home. I did not like conflict, so I would leave when the tension started. The beach was terrific; it had brilliant white sand that was very smooth and hot in the summer. There was always activity; people lined up at the pizza places for a slice and a coke. During the day, you could see people walking or riding bikes, carrying beach towels and picnic baskets. There were pavilions along the waterfront, some round and some rectangular; people would gather in the day's heat to escape the sun. Sometimes in the summer, bands would come and play in the pavilions. Pizza places sold pizza by the slice, and the smell of hot, fresh pizza filled the air and the smell of the saltwater and the waves crashing to the shore. There were rides, a roller coaster, a tilt-a-whirl, and bumper cars. But my absolute favorite thing of all was the carousel. Of course, it had horses, other animals, and carriages painted in brilliant colors.

I would go there every chance I got. They played a song over the speakers called "Somewhere My Love," also known as Lara's Theme from Dr. Zhivago. It was a haunting song, yet I would sit across the street to listen to the music and daydream about the next ride. The stretch of beach we hung out on was about a mile long, and about halfway down was a bathhouse, where people could go to shower after a day in the saltwater before going home for the night. The bathhouse was across the street from the police station. I stayed close to that area as it felt safe. I would spend many days walking the length of that stretch of the beach, rain or shine, anything to keep from being at home.

My grandmother was a shopper and a walker; I had to run to keep up whenever I walked with her anywhere. One day at breakfast, she came out and was having her tea when she told me to tell my mother that I was going with her for the day and would not be going to school. So she took me to Boston on the train. I spent the day trailing after her from one department store to another. Department stores were very tall buildings. Each floor was a different department, so we spent the day riding up and down in elevators, climbing stairs, and picking one or two items in each place. The crowds were excellent, though it was primarily women, each going from one store to the next, searching for the best bargain. It was loud, and we moved quickly; it felt like a race to get the next sale item before someone else. It was dollar days, and there were sales on everything, everywhere.

Around midday, we stopped for lunch. Wendy's was a brand new restaurant then, and my grandmother had heard that they had the best chili. After lunch, we still had more things to buy, so it was back to running after my grandmother again, squeezing into elevators that creaked and groaned until nearly dark. Finally, down to the last item, we stopped at Jordan Marsh's Basement; she left me and all her packages sitting on the steps to get that one item. When she returned, I was asleep on the steps, surrounded by those packages. When we got home, my mom was pretty upset as she had no idea where I was because she did not remember me telling her I was going shopping with Grandma.

I helped with chores around the house and kept an eye on my siblings. One evening, my grandmother asked me to load the dishwasher; being the smart-mouthed kid, I said no. It was a joke; I had every intention of doing it, but they did not take it as a joke. My grandfather sent me to my room, where he came up, unplugged my radio, and used the cord to spank me.

There was a church on the street behind our home. So the kids from the neighborhood and I would play stickball in the street, a game called Old Lady Witch on the steps to the church, and hide and seek in the field behind the church. The area was pretty swampy; there were cattails taller than us. There was a field behind our house that would get filled with water and freeze in the winter, and we would ice skate on it. Like the skaters I saw on TV, I used to daydream about being in the Olympics as a figure skater. They were beautiful and graceful and seemed to move effortlessly across the ice. As a child, I wanted to be anyone but who I was because I thought that everyone else was better than me. I felt that if I were someone famous, people would like me, and I wouldn't be an oddball.

My mom spent a lot of time going out at night, so I didn't see her very often, spending most of my time with my grandparents. Sometimes I would sneak downstairs after everyone was and watch Johnny Carson, Red Skelton, Lawrence Welk, or whatever Western my grandfather was watching. I never needed much sleep even then.

I was in the third grade. My sister, Patricia, was in first grade and not doing well. At first, her inability to comprehend the lessons got attributed to the divorce and laziness, so she repeated first grade. One day she stayed after school for extra help; I went to the classroom to wait for her, only to see the teacher strike her hand with a ruler. That kind of thing was allowed back then, but I was responsible for my sister, and no one was supposed to hit her. I got angry and took my sister out of school.

Like every school, we had our share of bullies because we were new, quiet, and different—we were targets. This particular day was not the day for them to come after us, but they did, and I had to protect my sister. We were nearly home when they surrounded us; I sent my sister home to get my grandfather. One of the girls pushed me, and I swung blindly, knocking one of the girls to the ground, and I ran home. A few hours later, the girl's mother came to my house and started yelling at my grandfather about hitting her daughter. My grandfather explained that her daughter hit me, and the lady cussed at him and told her to leave. Later, when the tempers calmed, I told my grandparents about what had happened, and the teacher was hitting my sister. My sister never went back to public school; doctors discovered that she had a form of epilepsy that kept her from learning beyond a certain level.

That incident caused my second trip to the principal's office; I had to tell on the teacher for hitting my sister and for the girls who picked on us. The bullies continued to harass me, so I started taking a different route to and from school since I usually walked past their houses. I began to withdraw from my friends after that. I learned to avoid everyone or not go anywhere alone. When trouble comes, the lesson I learned is to run or avoid it, which would carry me well into adulthood.

I had a secret life, the life I never told anyone back then. A man lived a couple of houses away; he was a family friend; occasionally, I would run errands; his wife was sick. I would get cigarettes, milk, or stamps, simple things that he didn't want to leave his wife alone to get for them. Finally, after about a year or so, he would ask me to come into the house, and I was ten. He began hugging me, touching me, or making me sit on his lap; I didn't know why, but it made me uncomfortable, and I made excuses to stop going.

I stopped going out; I went to school, church, and the library. Since I was hanging around so much, my grandfather thought I should learn to mix his nightly highball. During family parties, I was the bartender; we had a lot of parties and a big family. My grandfather had six siblings, and my grandmother also had six siblings, but only one lived in Massachusetts. My grandfather told me I needed to know what they tasted like, so I sampled every other drink to ensure it was right. It was also my job to clean up in the evening, and after events, somehow I thought it was a good idea to finish the leftover drinks rather than pour them out. My grandmother would often fall asleep with her glass in her hand; I will never know how she never spilled it. After she fell asleep, my sister and I would make a game out of trying to get my grandmother's drink out of her hand. I didn't know then that I was building my tolerance for alcohol because I didn't get drunk; at least, I don't think I did. I didn't realize this was wrong or unusual, and I did not talk about it.

For the next couple of years, I kept to myself, got good grades, looked after my siblings while mom was away or asleep, and read a lot.

The Breaking Phase

During my sixth-grade year, I had to have my tonsils removed a week after school started; Mom took me to the hospital, left me there, and went on a date. When I got home that weekend, there was a big argument between my mom, her siblings, and my grandparents, and we had to leave. We moved into a big house around the corner from my school, another one-room schoolhouse that would close at the end of the school year. Mom was gone a lot in the evenings, and the landlord disapproved, so we moved again. I had so much trouble making friends with girls that I started hanging around with the boys on the basketball court by this time. I enjoyed watching them play; sometimes, they would ask me to join in, and I was terrible. I would go to the court to read since we were too far from the beach. We moved into a basement apartment about a mile away from my grandparents, two blocks from the beach, and I changed schools. The apartment building was across the street from a church on one side and a cemetery and park on the other side.

The doctor discovered that Patricia and David had epilepsy, which caused them to have learning disabilities, and they got sent to special schools. Patricia went to school and came home every day, while David went to school on Monday and came home on Friday. David had an obvious disability; he could not speak well for his age and was not developing. However, while Patricia was a stutterer, she had no apparent signs of disability. Then when she was about twelve or thirteen, she had a grand mal seizure; we found out she had been having petit mal seizures since she was two.

My mother's boyfriend lived upstairs; he was disabled and a heroin addict. He had a hobby of building and racing gas-powered

RC cars. She spent most of her time with him leaving us alone downstairs. One weekend Mom and her boyfriend went to a race and left me in charge of the other kids. David was a pest and was always trying to provoke me; this weekend was no exception; the only problem was I was already angry at my mom for leaving us alone all weekend. He poked and prodded me until I snapped, and in a blind rage, I grabbed the nearest thing I could find, a dog leash, and I hit him until my sister pulled me off him. No one told on me, so Mom did not know.

On Monday, when he went back to school, the principal called my mother, and I got called to the school for a conference, they asked what happened, and my mother did not know what they were talking about, but I did. They called child protective services, and my brother lived with my grandparents until he graduated from school. My aunt tried to get custody of me, my sister, and Michael and got denied. I learned to cook and babysit, and I would get Michael from the babysitter when I got home from school. When I had money from babysitting, I would go to the grocery store and get meat, usually ground beef, since that was all I knew how to cook. Most of our food came from a warehouse that gave commodities to people on welfare. I still am not a fan of scrambled eggs or canned meat.

So I came to a new neighborhood, new school, and new people, and even though I still kept to myself, I began meeting people and going back to the beach. But unfortunately, my isolation, love of reading, having disabled siblings, being an honor roll student, and being on welfare made me a target for the bullies again.

I finished sixth grade and moved to junior high school. In seventh grade, my reading finally began to benefit me when I completed the required reading assignment in the first week. After that, the teacher asked for a book report once a week for the rest of the year. The struggle started with math. It did not make sense to me, and as hard as I tried, I couldn't get it. My teachers gave me credit for attempting as they could see I was not good at math.

I took Michael to the beach for pizza; there was one place where the owners would let him sit up on the counter so he could watch what they were doing. I still went to church, confessing and telling the priest all I had done. Mainly, I used foul language, sneaked out, and occasionally lied about where I was or with who. I started hanging out with the neighborhood boys, playing basketball, going to the arcades, watching the sunrise on the beach, sneaking out of the apartment, and smoking cigarettes. I felt like a kid for a change.

Mom started noticing that I was gone a lot and had too many friends that were not girls. She stayed downstairs with us for a few weeks to monitor my behavior. She also decided that since I would hang out with boys, she would get me a boyfriend and introduce me to a friend's brother. We got along pretty well, but he was a few years older and decided I was too immature. We would stay at my house watching TV; he tried to kiss me or touch me a couple of times, but I wouldn't let him. I recently discovered movies like *The Mummy*, *Dracula*, and *The Werewolf* and actors like Bella Lugosi, Vincent Price, and Lon Chaney were my favorites. He liked wrestling, and I didn't like the violence. So after a few months, we broke up.

I had a crush on a boy at school, and I thought he felt the same way. So we started hanging out; he would walk me home, carry my books, and go to the basketball court together. He asked if he could come over after dinner to watch TV, and I agreed. That night he came over with several of his friends; I told him that I could not allow them in because I would get in trouble. He pushed the door open, and they all came into the apartment. He asked if he could talk to me in my room alone, and I said it wasn't a good idea, but he took my hand and led me to my room. He told me he liked me and started kissing and touching me. When I tried to say no, the other boys came in, held me down, and started taking my clothes off; when I tried to argue and refuse, someone hit me, and when I cried out, someone shoved their penis in my mouth. I closed my eyes and cried as they touched me all over and raped me repeatedly. I don't know how long they were there when my mother came in; she started yelling. She told me I was a whore for letting them touch me. Then she grounded me.

I tried to tell her what had happened, and she said I was a liar and a whore and needed to stay in my room. I felt ashamed, guilty, and dirty. I cried myself to sleep for a long time, months. After this,

I started taking hot baths rather than showers. I would get the water so hot it made my skin turn red, and I would scrub every inch of my body. Yet no matter how hard I scrubbed, I did not feel clean.

The next day at school, everyone knew what happened except they heard that I invited them and asked for it to happen. I shut down and would not speak to anyone; I was humiliated, embarrassed, and ashamed. I stopped going anywhere except school and church because I got grounded from then and for the whole summer; this happened the spring after I turned twelve.

About a month after school let out for the summer, I was reading on my bed when someone knocked on my bedroom window. It was a boy I knew through the boyfriend my mom had chosen for me, though I didn't know him well. We sat and talked out the window for a while, and then he asked if I wanted to walk the beach with him, and I did because I was mad at my mom for leaving me alone. Michael and Patricia were upstairs with my mom, and David was at school. So I went with him; we walked to the arcade and hung out there for a while, and then as it was starting to get dark, I was starting to get scared; I told him I needed to go home. He said he wanted to watch the sunset; I told him I had to get home before Mom noticed I was gone. He asked me to wait a few more minutes, and he would make sure I got home before dark.

We were sitting on the breaker wall when he suggested we go closer to the water. We climbed down onto the rocks when he turned to me and kissed me. I told him no and tried to get away. Instead he pulled a knife, held it to my throat, told me to be quiet, and raped me. I walked home by myself; I felt broken, ashamed, dirty, and ugly. I prayed, yet I did not think God cared about me. The rape changed me in many ways; I began to isolate myself, changed how I dressed, and wore only long pants and long sleeve shirts, even in the summer. I no longer went swimming and stayed away from the water. I got home, and my mom was waiting for me; we got into a big argument, and the first thing the following day, after she went back upstairs, I ran away.

I stayed on strangers' couches for almost a week, hung out with people I didn't know, and smoked pot. Then one day I was at the arcade, and I heard my mom's car coming, and the people I was with hid me behind the Skee-Ball machine. The next day one of the people I was with convinced me that I needed to go home as living on the streets was unsuitable for a child, so I went home.

The new school year had begun, and before I could go back to any of my classes, I had to talk to the principal. He told me I was a horribly disrespectful child and needed to set a better example for my siblings and treat my mother better. After that, I was so ashamed back in my classes I could not look at anyone, and no one spoke to me, and I withdrew into myself. I started wishing I was invisible, or that I could go to sleep and not wake up, that everyone would be better off if I were gone. But I still went to church because something kept telling me that I could learn to be a better person if I kept going to church; there were not enough Hail Mary's and Our Father's I could say that would make me feel forgiven.

Soon after, in the fall of 1972, around Thanksgiving, my mother realized that I was pregnant. She was angry; she accused me of being a whore. She told me I would have an abortion, then I got angry. I told her I couldn't have an abortion because I would get kicked out of the church. I knew I could not raise a child my age but could give it up for adoption. She laughed at me and told me that God could not forgive my actions. Then she asked who the father was; I told her what happened all those months ago, for the first time, about the boy with the knife. She never knew about the boy from school.

She called the police, and a detective came to our house. He was a big intimidating man who made me relive every graphic detail of what he had done to me. I had to say things I had never spoken before, using unfamiliar words; I was so afraid and humiliated that I could barely speak above a whisper. He asked me what I had done to provoke the boy, how I dressed, and what I said to make him think I wanted it. Then he told me that rape was a victimless crime; at the time, I did not know what that meant. He said that in "he said, she said" cases, no one was at fault. Therefore, there was no victim.

The next day my mother dropped me off at the hospital to have an abortion. They found that I was six months pregnant, and a normal abortion would not be possible for me. They would have to induce labor, and I would have to give birth. I did not know what they were talking about, and I was too afraid, ashamed, and discouraged to ask questions. I lay there, crying while they performed the procedure; it would be many years before I found out what had happened. I was in the hospital for two days. My mom's boyfriend picked me up and reprimanded me the whole way home for bringing all this stress on my mother. He told me what an awful, disrespectful child I was and that now that I had given birth to a child. I was no longer a child, and I better grow up. I barely heard what he said; I was in pain, inside and out.

I got home and went to bed, pulling the covers over my head and praying to die. After two days, my mom came into my room to tell me that I could no longer feel sorry for myself and needed to get up for school. I told her I was cold and in a lot of pain. She got angry, saying it was an excuse to get out of school and that I needed to face what I had done. I will never forget the words she said to me, "You made your bed; now lay in it." I got up and started to get ready for school when she realized that I didn't look right; I had a fever of 103. She immediately took me to the hospital, telling me how inconvenient I was to her and her plans for the day; I had a kidney infection.

When I finally recovered physically, I went to the church to confess; the priest met me at the door and told me I was not welcome. I was devastated; now, my fear was confirmed; that God didn't want me. I was garbage. My mother sent me to see a psychiatrist in Boston. I took the train into Boston and had to walk across the Commons to get to the office. During this time, there were many people hanging around in the Commons who used drugs and played music. I went to two sessions, and the lady kept asking me why I hated my mother so much that I would act out in such an ugly manner.

The case made it before a judge, which is where we found out that the boy had a pending case in another court. I was not his first. The lawyer asked my mother what she wanted in the way of punishment. She responded that he be held responsible for all the hospital bills. Somehow I made it through the rest of the school year. The following year, I would be in high school, and no one would know what I was.

My mother's boyfriend had friends who needed a babysitter for their two small children a week after school. I was to go live with them in Roxbury for the summer. I never knew their names. I was to call them sir and ma'am. The lady worked the second shift, and the man worked days. He told me the boys needed to take their naps late, so they were asleep when he came home to unwind before taking care of them after work.

One day he came into my room after work and began touching and talking to me. He seemed very kind at first. The next day he started feeling me under my clothes, and I tried to tell him I didn't like it. He told me it was my payment for taking care of his children, so I cried while he touched me. I closed my eyes and went away, so I could not feel what he did. A week later, my mother called to say my dad was coming to take me to Michigan for the summer. God rescued me, even when I no longer believed.

Further Destruction

My first impression of my stepmother, Ruth, was that she was a charming person and cared about me. There was nothing spectacular about that summer until the last week when Dad and Ruth sat me down and said they wanted to talk to me about something. They asked me if I would consider living with them permanently. I agreed at once as I saw it as an opportunity to escape the city, the horror, and no one knew me; I could be invisible.

The day we put my siblings on a plane back to Massachusetts, my dad, Ruth, and I sat down again. This time it was not good news. Dad told me that he knew everything I had done, my lies, and my disrespectful behavior toward my mother. My mother told him that I had made up stories about being raped and hurt. He said that behavior was unacceptable in his house. I had a clean slate, and it was up to me to keep it that way.

To ensure I was behaving, I had chores I had to do every day to earn time to do what I wanted. So every morning I got up before everyone else, made lunches, dusted, vacuumed, and cleaned the bathroom. I then took a shower and woke everyone up for school and work. I had two stepbrothers who were not thrilled at a new older sister, and they found ways to let me know every chance they got. They would call me names, blame me for things they did and lie about me to make me do their chores. Since I felt that I was a horrible person, I did not complain; I did what they wanted, working as hard as possible to be good in all I did.

I was a straight-A student; I did all my chores and followed the rules. Dad decided that I was going to be a secretary. He said I would never amount to anything and needed to take care of myself as no one would ever love or want me because I was fat and ugly. So I took classes geared toward secretarial school; I despised and excelled at them, pleasing my dad because I got good grades. I didn't even try to make friends; I kept to myself and rarely spoke.

A few of the girls tried to talk to me, but I did not know what to say to them. One day a boy whose locker was next to mine asked why I never smiled; I told him I had no reason to smile. He seemed to take that as a challenge because he would talk to me every day and try to make me smile. One day, I came home from school, and my dad told me that I could not talk to the boy anymore because his family was migrant workers. I had no idea what difference it made, but I did what they told me. That was my first year in high school; my sophomore year was not great.

I am terrible at math, numbers make no sense to me, and I had to take algebra. When I came home with a C, my dad requested a conference with the teacher. He told the teacher that I was lazy and stupid, needed more work, and pushed harder. The teacher disagreed; he told my dad that I needed to receive a passing grade and put me in study hall since I had no aptitude for math. That teacher did not follow my dad's recommendations; he passed me with a C and put me in study hall. He was the first person who stood up for me even if no one knew; I will never forget him. After that, things at home got worse. I did my chores, went to work for Ruth's dad in the field picking and orchards, and worked diligently at school, yet it was never enough. I picked asparagus in the spring, cherries in the summer, and apples in the fall. I gave all the money I earned to my dad because he said it was to pay for my room and board.

I had made a few friends at school, so I thought, and got invited to a birthday party. It was supposed to be a slumber party. My dad and Ruth went with me, telling the girl's parents that I could not be trusted and could not spend the night. Sometime later, on my sixteenth birthday, I asked if I could have a slumber party. They agreed, I had a pretty good night, and I thought I had finally made some friends. The following day, when the girls had left, I got in trouble because we stayed up too late and made too much noise. I was grounded for two weeks and told I could not have friends over again.

Most of those girls never spoke to me again, and that experience taught me that I was a worthless, horrible person.

Then a letter came, and the police explorers wanted me; my dad said I must have lied on the test because they would not want me if they knew what a horrible liar I was.

My dad told me often that I was stupid, fat, and ugly and that no one would ever want or love me. Then my dad brought a man home one day and told me I could date him. The intention was for me to date him through high school and then marry him. He was active Army, he was twenty-one, home on leave, and we were allowed to spend time together away from the family and with the family. One night we went to square dance; I accidentally touched him on his thigh on the way home. He told my dad about it when we got home. My dad gave him his belt and told the man to spank me with it, and then I was not allowed to see him again.

Toward the end of the school year, I came home, and Ruth said we needed to talk. She told me that someone had seen me smoking at the grocery store across the street from the school. I told her it wasn't me, but she did not believe me. I got grounded to my room, and they confronted me again when my dad came home. I was not there, yet they did not believe me, and there was no way for me to prove that I was telling the truth. They took me to confront the lady who claimed to have seen me and apologize for calling her a liar. I could not do what they asked because I wasn't lying; the lady made a mistake. My dad spanked me with his belt when we got home for embarrassing them, and I was to stay in my room until I could tell the truth.

A week passed, and I got confronted again; I stood my ground. Dad was furious; he stood up so fast that his chair flew across the room; he grabbed me by the throat, pushed me into the refrigerator, and punched me. Then dad told me to go for a walk to cool off, and I did. I walked all night, crossing fields, orchards, and roads until I came to my paternal grandparent's house, the next town over. They woke up to find me sitting on their doorstep with a black eye. I told them everything that happened, they made some phone calls, and I was sent back to my dad's house for two weeks until we went to court.

That was a miserable two weeks. They told me that when I left, I was not allowed to take anything with me except my clothes; I was to stay in my room and not have any further influence over the boys. The story I was to tell was that I got a black eye from an accident when helping Ruth with dinner. When we got to court, the judge asked my dad what he wanted to do with me. Dad stood up and told the judge to lock me up because I was incorrigible.

My uncle stood up in the back of the room and said they would take me. So I became a state ward and finished the school year with my cousins. My aunt came down from the upper peninsula in Michigan and took me to live with her. My aunt was a remarkable woman; she was a solid Christian and the kindest person. She tried to help me, teach me to live a different life, and introduce me to a God-led life; I believed I was beyond help.

She took me to church, she tried to teach me how to live a Christian life, and she did not believe I was garbage though I was not convinced. I paid close attention in church, got involved in Sunday school, choir, and the youth group, went through the motions, and did not believe there was any hope for me. I was a round peg in a square hole; I did not fit anywhere. Life went well for me; I did well in school, began to socialize, and started dating one of the neighbor boys. His mother heard about my past, decided I was not good enough for her son, and made him break up with me.

We moved back down to Hart, Michigan, near summer after school got out. They had bought a big farmhouse, and I thought it was beautiful. There was a barn and the most extensive garden I had ever seen. They split the garden into three sections one for flowers, one for vegetables, and one for corn. They got chickens and a couple of goats that I learned how to raise. Feeding the chickens and gathering eggs wasn't so bad, but milking the goats was a real challenge at first.

For a few months, I got to be an average teenager. We went roller skating occasionally; sometimes, we would go to the drive-in. Most of the time, we stayed close to home; there was a pond down the road we would go to hang out. My cousin was dating someone she met through a friend, and he introduced me to his cousin so we could go on dates with them. We began dating, going to movies, youth groups, and family dinners. One night after a movie, he convinced me to have sex with him; I liked him and thought that if I didn't, he would leave me. My dad's words rang in my ears that no one would want or love me. So I gave in to him because he said he loved me; I became pregnant; I was seventeen and still in high school. When I told my aunt, she was as angry as I had ever seen her, and the words she said haunted me for many years. She said, "After all we have done for you, and this is how you repay us."

The Descent into Darkness

Two weeks after my eighteenth birthday in 1978, I was married to a man I didn't know if I loved and pregnant with a child I had no idea how to raise. We moved into an apartment in town; he joined the Air Force and left for basic training while I stayed and finished school. After graduation, I lived with my in-laws until the baby was born, which turned out to be twenty-seven days later. When my daughter was a month old, I was on a plane about to be a military wife, mother, and homemaker with no one to turn to; my family had disowned me, or so I believed. Our first duty station was Nellis Air Force Base in Las Vegas, Nevada, in 1978. I arrived at the end of July and was nearly overwhelmed with the heat. The day I landed in Las Vegas, it was 100 degrees in the shade, and we went for a walk. He found a one-and-a-half-bedroom trailer that we stayed in for several months. It wasn't long before I got pregnant again; my husband decided he didn't want any more children with me, and I got my tubes tied the day my second daughter was born.

After that, we occasionally began going to parties and socializing with other couples. Most weekends, my husband went out with his friends as he said I was repulsive to him because I was fat and ugly. I wasn't old enough to go out with him, and I would beg him to stay home with the girls and me. He worked the second shift, so I saw him before he went to work in the afternoon. Sometimes, we would go to the mountains or Lake Mead though not often as he was ashamed to be seen with me. We would go to Circus Circus; it was the only casino I could go to and take the girls. Upstairs designed for children, they would have magic acts for the kids while the parents gambled. I learned how to be a mom; I learned how to cook, clean, be a wife, and run a home with two small children.

I wasn't very good at being a homemaker. The house was never clean enough, the meals were too bland, and I didn't watch the children closely enough; my husband told me almost daily. One day I was cleaning, and I heard my youngest start to scream. I ran out to the living room to find that the older girl had shut the door on her sister's fingers to keep her from going outside. I told a neighbor to call my husband and ask him to meet me at the hospital. I was terrified and thought that I was going to lose my children. At that time, the issue of child abuse was becoming prevalent, and since my husband had told me I was a horrible mother, I was afraid. As it turned out, the doctor said that nothing got broken and that these things happen a lot with a two-year-old in the house.

I began to drink socially. My marriage was in trouble, and I was scared. I did not know what I would do if I got divorced; I had already shamed my family and knew I could not go home. My husband thought that a change of scenery would help us work through the problems in our relationship. So at the end of 1980, we received orders to Anchorage, Alaska; we moved in January 1981. Talk about a change; we went from the desert to the tundra!

We had a fresh start, new people, new playgrounds, and new ways of doing things. I got a job working at the daycare center on base. I worked with four- to six-year-olds. I loved that job and wanted to stay, but my husband said I didn't make enough money and needed to get a job off base. So I worked at Chuck E. Cheese as a birthday hostess. I loved it, it was fast-paced, and I got to work with children. I loved the noise, chaos, and people. I made some good friends. We had a good time at work, though I never told any of them about what was going on at home.

A lesson I learned early on stayed with me, keeping secrets. Soon we began socializing with married people, settling into a different lifestyle. I did not like these changes, but he was my husband, the head of the house. He paid the bills, and I did what he wanted, even if I didn't like it. I was entirely dependent on him. We would play cards, watch movies, have barbeques, go camping and fishing, panning for gold, and four-wheeling. I learned how to pan for gold and shoot a revolver. However, I was not allowed to hunt or fish because I was there as the camp cook and a girl. Then something changed; I don't know when or how it happened, but we were at a friend's house one night, and they put on a pornographic movie. I was utterly humiliated and embarrassed. He would try to have sex with me during the film, and I would silently cry while he touched me. I wanted to leave, but my husband refused, so we stayed and returned several more times.

Then one night, he suggested we host the movie and have other couples come over to watch. I said no, but he was my husband, and I did it because he wanted to. We had been drinking, and had I been sober enough to refuse, our marriage would have ended then; it did not. When the movie was over, he told me to sit on the lap of one of his friends and gave his friend permission to do whatever he wanted to me, and he did. I felt cheap, used, degraded, and humiliated.

Swinging caused several arguments between my husband and me until it finally stopped. He started going out without me again. Even though I still didn't have any hope, I started going back to church; I searched for something though I didn't know what. I started in-home businesses like Tupperware, Amway, etc. I wasn't successful; I am not a salesperson.

One night after another unsuccessful Tupperware party, my husband came home drunk. And after telling me what a worthless, fat, ugly loser no one would ever want I was, he went to bed. My friend from church was there and heard what he said. She told me that I did not have to live like that, that God did not mean for me to get treated that way. I was astounded. Was that true, a way out? I left the next day.

After a week, he called me and said he would change and that if I came home, he would buy me a microwave, and I went back. It did not take long for the old behaviors to come back, and this time, when I left, I took the girls with me; I stayed gone. He filed for divorce and told me to be at the courthouse at a specific time and date. I arrived on a rainy August afternoon. I got out of the car, and he came across the parking lot and handed me the signed divorce papers and custody agreement. He had me declared legally unfit to care for my children, and he got awarded full custody. He used my job at Chuck E. Cheese to prove that I could not support my children. I never set foot in the courtroom. I went back to my apartment, and I got drunk, little did I know that I would barely draw a sober breath for the next seven years.

I married husband number two, who I met in a bar within a year in 1984. I worked two jobs; I started working at Village Inn a few graveyard shifts a week. It was too little too late, but I did not understand that in my drunken mind. Eventually that job interfered with my drinking, and I quit. Then new management came into Chuck E. Cheese, and I got fired. I had been working there for about five years, and by the time I got home, the owner had called me and rehired me. I didn't work there much longer after that. I knew the new management team wanted me gone, so I got a job at the Godfather's Pizza, located behind Chuck E. Cheese. We moved to three or four apartments during that time, and we spent nearly every night in the clubs, drinking, and dancing. I had a car when we first got together, and one day, when my children were visiting, we were hit by a drunk driver who had no insurance.

The car was totaled, and we could not afford a new one, so we bought bicycles. I worked at Round Table Pizza, so I rode my bike across town about twenty miles a day. Without a car, we rode bikes everywhere. We decided to start going to church because we were partying excessively and thought we needed to straighten out our lives so we could spend more time with my children. We went to church for a couple of Sundays, and some people from the church came to our house with a book of bylaws, which was nearly a thousand pages long, that we would have to follow to be members of that church. They wanted us to change the music we listened to, which at the time was primarily heavy metal. We never went back to that church.

The drinking and partying got more intense, and I became increasingly depressed. Every area of my life got darker, more reckless. I was drinking to oblivion and beyond; he introduced me to cocaine; until then I was strictly a drinker who used marijuana occasionally. I was allowing my husband to abuse me sexually. He found it exciting to share me with his friends and enable them to watch and find objects to use on me. Most of the time, I was so drunk or high I couldn't have objected or fought him off if I had thought of it: I didn't.

Until one night, he decided to replace his penis inside me with a revolver; unloaded, all the same, it terrified me, and the more scared I was, the more aroused he became. I was a sideshow for him and his friends. I was so lost and hopeless that I no longer cared; there were times when I wished the gun were loaded.

Around this time, my first husband told me that he had orders to Tampa, Florida, and he would be taking the girls with him.

My husband brought home a new friend and used harder drugs with him. This man was rough and had no respect for women. My husband had been changing for a while in how he treated me. His friend commented that men should beat women daily. I told him to leave, and my husband went with him. We later found out that this man had raped and murdered his sister and two small nieces. When my husband came home, I asked him where he had been. He grabbed me by the hair and slammed my head into the arm of the couch. He had hit me before, but it was the last. I divorced him immediately after in 1986.

I worked at an auto-parts company and had a car, but I eventually became homeless because I couldn't afford an apartment. Finally I found a trailer and was able to stay there for a few months until the owner decided to move into it himself. After that, I slept on couches at other people's houses.

During the time between marriages, I drifted all over the state, got involved in a CB group, and went to bars more often by myself. I spent hours in the evening talking to people all over town. It helped with the loneliness to have someone to talk to in the late nights when I couldn't sleep and couldn't afford to go out drinking. I finally made friends. Once in a while, we would get together for coffee or dinner. We went on picnics, camping, and sightseeing together. We tagged along with a local motorcycle club on the Toys for Tots ride one year. One of the group members had a van and carried all the camping gear and food for the trip. We rode from Anchorage to Fairbanks. Once in Fairbanks, we parted company with the club and went off on our own to explore. We found a rest area in North Pole, Alaska, and stopped for lunch.

I would drive down the coast to McHugh Creek or Kenai just to drive. I would go to these picturesque sights to find peace. I would slowly walk through the woods and just listen. I don't know what I was listening for or what I expected to find. What I did find was peace. Sometimes a group of us would have picnics and go hiking. I went camping with friends and alone. I isolated more and more, not wanting to be around people, so I would sit in the woods or near a river simply to be alone. I got to see the Aurora Borealis many times up there; that is the most spectacular sight. Sometimes coming home from the bar in the winter, I would see the shimmering lights dancing across the sky and think about the tremendous power that created such breathtaking beauty and wonder. It hurt to see such exquisite beauty and know that I was so ugly inside.

When the second marriage ended, I decided not to get married. I was twenty-six and had already married and divorced twice; I stayed by myself for two years. I made a trip to Portage Glacier several times. I enjoyed the drive, and there are no words to describe the breathtaking beauty of an active glacier. One of the things I learned during this time was that driving was an excellent time to find peace. Driving was the only time I felt like I had any control over my life. I moved every few months, changed jobs almost every year, went out with anyone who would give me a second look, and was a party girl. Drinking, dancing, sex, and a few experiments with drugs became my life. I did not give God a second thought for quite some time; why would I? I was a failure, a total loss, with no hope of redemption, so who cared.

Then I met husband number three in 1988; I didn't know it then. He moved in with me two weeks later. He introduced me to speed (amphetamines); I wasn't interested in making any changes; I wasn't looking for anything more than someone to help pay the bills. The only problem was that he wasn't working, and I supported him. I no longer cared about living; I merely wanted to exist. Little did I know that was all about to change drastically. So we continued to drink, use drugs, and dance, but the sex with strangers stopped. I wanted a sugar daddy, and he needed fixing. We were both wrong.

After a few months, he said he had a stop to make while we ran errands in a borrowed car. I was waiting in the car, and he came back in handcuffs. I learned then that he was on parole and had to go back to jail for a year because he wasn't supposed to be drinking and using drugs. It was then that it occurred to me to ask him why he had been in prison in the first place. He went to jail, and I went home, lost, confused, and uncertain; I continued to drink, quit going to the clubs, and was working and drinking. I put my life on hold for a year. My friends and his family told me to walk away, that he was not worth me giving up my life and that I would regret it. During that year, I lost my apartment because I was supporting him. I still did not have a car, yet he insisted I visit him every week; it was an hour's drive away.

I would borrow a car or get rides from friends. He had a friend who managed an apartment complex, and they rented me an apartment. I had also lost my job, so the apartment manager found me a position in his store, a sex shop. This place was scary; most of the customers were men, and there were booths in the back where people could watch pornographic movies. I worked the graveyard shift, so many people who came in were intoxicated. I worked there for about a month when I heard someone pull up outside one quiet night. He came inside, pointed a gun at me, handcuffed me, told me not to touch the alarm, and gave up the money in the register. I had triggered the alarm before he told me not to as it was a button on the floor; it was a silent alarm connected to the police department. After he left, the police came, with their guns drawn, got me out of the handcuffs, and waited with me until the owner showed up.

One night, I came home after being out drinking to see the building on fire. I had to stay in that apartment for a month without water or electricity. Then I found a little cabin in downtown Anchorage through a friend. It was cheap. I moved in there and stayed there for a few months. One winter night, I came home from work, and a man came out of my house with my baseball bat. I ran!

I made it to a payphone and called a friend who called the police. When the police came, they discovered that the guy had been watching me for quite some time. There were six inches of snow on the ground except for the length of my house in the back. I was back to couch surfing for about a week before finding an apartment.

I found a basement apartment a few months before he came home. A month before he came home, he requested placement and got granted a rehabilitation center. He was sober, and I was a drunken mess, full of fear, insecurity, guilt, and shame. When he told me that his counselor recommended that I go to Al-Anon, I went willingly, thinking I would help him. Wow was I wrong.

A Shimmer of Light

I walked into that meeting terrified; I knew nothing about recovery, Al-Anon, or Alcoholics Anonymous. I listened to the people talk and wanted to hide; I couldn't get out of there fast enough. They were talking about me. Later, I realized they spoke of the alcoholic in their lives, the shoe fit, and I wore it. I left that meeting feeling guilty, ashamed, embarrassed, and desperate.

It was dark outside, and I was on the other side of town from home. I came to a crossroads and checked for traffic when I heard an unmistakable audible voice say, "You're an alcoholic." I did not move; I turned slowly to look because I thought someone was in the car with me. But there was no one; there was not another car or person anywhere near me. I was terrified; I was hyperalert, checking mirrors and the surrounding area. I was shaking uncontrollably, could barely breathe, and near panicked. I could not go to my apartment; I was scared. I went to a neighbor's, and when I walked in, she could tell I was afraid. She offered me a drink, and I said no, that I needed to stop drinking and stop living the way I was living.

I realized that I had become a person I did not like. She asked me if I was serious, and I was; she went into the other room and came out with a book and handed it to me. It was the book Alcoholics Anonymous. I was shocked; there was a woman I had drank and used drugs with for several years, and I had no idea that she had been a member of AA. I asked her about it, and she told me that she had tried to get it many years before, but it didn't work for her.

The next day, December 17, 1989, I was sitting in a meeting of Alcoholics Anonymous. I showed up at that first meeting, held in one of the bars I used to drink at, a nervous wreck and scared. I was afraid to speak, and when they mentioned God, I thought they would make me leave when they found out that God didn't want anything to do with me. They told me I had to attend ninety meetings in ninety days, read the big book, get a sponsor, and use them. I followed every suggestion because I thought that my life depended on it. I went to the ninety meetings, got a book, and went home and read every word. I had no idea what I was reading and did not understand how that would keep me from drinking. I did not drink or use any substance, and I learned to follow directions. They called them suggestions; they were a lifeline I did not have previously.

Since then, I have not found it necessary to take a drink or a drug. Does that mean that my life sober has been sunshine and unicorns? No! Did I suddenly start making better choices? Nope! Did I become financially responsible? No, I did not. Was I willing to believe that God would magically make all the wrongs in my life right? Not then, I didn't. I still did not think that God wanted anything to do with me. Did I finally lose my fear, insecurity, anxiety, guilt, and shame? Not that either. Was I finally ready to come out of my shell and let my light shine? Not even close. As close as I could come to God, then was a Group Of Drunks.

I put my faith and trust in them because they had something I wanted, and it looked vastly different than what I had. I went to meetings every day, and one of the women pulled me aside one day and asked me a few questions that I do not remember. I was only a few days, maybe a month, sober and still in a fog and terrified. She asked if I wanted to be straight; I could only nod. I don't think I stopped crying for the first year or two I was sober. She gave me her address and told me to meet her there the next day. She would help me learn how to live sober. I did what she asked, went to her house, and cleaned her kitchen cabinets; I had no idea how that would keep me straight, but I was willing to do anything.

After hearing that voice in the car, I thought I was losing my mind and had better get help. Later I realized that I had not drunk that day, and it never crossed my mind either. When I was about a month or two sober, my then-boyfriend got out of treatment. He decided that we needed to move to Tacoma, Washington, because he did not think he could stay sober living in Alaska. I no longer felt that I had anything keeping me there, and I did not know I could stay sober without him. In addition, the move would bring me closer to my children.

Hence I agreed to go with him. So in August 1990, we loaded up our little Honda Civic with everything we owned and drove from Anchorage, Alaska, through Canada to Tacoma, Washington. We traveled through the Yukon Territory and British Columbia on the Al-Can Highway. We stopped twice a day to eat and slept in the car, in rest areas and parking lots most of the time. It was a beautiful trip; we saw lakes so crystal clear they were like glass. We were blessed with fantastic weather nearly down. At one point, we drove into a strong storm. The only way out was through. It was a little frightening to go through the driving rain. But watching as the rain receded and gave way to a glorious sunny day was incredible.

We made a few stops to enjoy the sights of a magnificent land-scape. I did not know that a forest ravaged by wildfire could be beautiful until I saw it. First we passed a couple of woods destroyed by wildfire, one recently extinguished. The burned trees stood still smoldering; the smell of burned wood hung in the air. A thin mist of smoke covered the ground. One had scorched years before and covered the ground with green The leafy plants rose among the burned trees. Next, we stopped at 100 Mile House, where we saw the world's largest cross-country skis. When we saw them, we stopped, the sun was rising, and they looked spectacular in the early morning light with a light fog covering everything. Finally, in one town, we stopped and watched a barrel race. A crowd had gathered, so we stopped; on a bridge across the river were several people with different colored barrels. While we watched, they tossed the barrels into the river below.

Eventually, we stopped at a campground near a lake about half-way down. As we drove in, we saw a cache, a tall structure used for storing meat to keep it out of reach of wildlife. We parked and met the proprietor, who gave us a tour of the different monuments and outbuildings. He had constructed an outdoor shower with hot and cold running water using barrels and tubes, including a shower cur-tain and a place to put towels, clothes, and toiletries. Then there was his-and-hers outhouse and, lastly, a three- or four-foot stack of empty alcohol bottles. He was forty years sober, which seemed unfathomable to us, as we had less than a year.

We finally arrived at his sister's house in Tacoma, who greeted us with a beer and asked us if we wanted one. We unloaded the car and found the nearest meeting as soon as possible. That was how we found Spanaway Hall and a whole new family and life. I was still afraid that they would make me leave if they found out all I had done. When I listened to people share, I would hear everything that told me I didn't belong because all I could hear were the differences. I went to meetings every day; I was there every time there was a meeting. I had to find a job, yet I could not figure out how to navigate life without drinking.

I soon found a job working as a delivery driver, so I worked days and went to meetings at night. I knew that I needed to find a sponsor, so I started listening to the women, and one day, someone told me to stop listening for the differences and listen for the similarities. I eventually chose a woman who seemed to have a story similar to mine. He did not like her and told me I could not ask her to sponsor me, so I did it anyway. That act of rebellion, standing up for myself, was the beginning of a journey I did not see coming. He said she didn't like men and would have a problem with us. But she had something I wanted, even though I did not know what it was, and I didn't care what he said. So we were working and going to meetings, and it wasn't long before we moved into our place. During our second year sober, he decided we needed to start going to church. I was hesitant at first, as the church thing had never really worked out well for me. Finally I agreed to give it a shot, though I had my doubts.

Since the day that priest told me I was not welcome at church when I was twelve, every time I walked into a church, I felt that every horrible thing I had ever done was on full display. I would never be good enough for God no matter what I did. We eventually got involved in the church and Sunday school; I joined the choir, becoming involved in church events. Soon after joining the church, he decided we should get baptized and be married, so we did. We were opposites; he wanted to be seen and heard, and I tried to hide in the shadows. When we would go to meetings or church, he would tell everyone everything that was going on with us, whether or not it was appropriate. I found myself embarrassed or humiliated a lot.

That was also the year my maternal grandmother passed away. One day I got a phone call from my mother saying that grandma was not doing well, and she wanted to see me. So I got on a plane and went back to Massachusetts for the second time in seventeen years. I had gone home on vacation for a couple of days before moving to Alaska. This time I went alone; I did not know what to expect, I was no longer the person I had been, but inside, I was still the scared little girl who had left all those years before. I had to face all the members of my family and some I did not know, and I had no idea how I was going to make it through.

The saving grace was my uncle. He brought his oldest son, who was thirteen, with him, and I spent as much time with my cousin. I always could relate better to children. I had been there a few days when I came out of the shower and found that my grandmother had passed away. A few days after the funeral, I was on a bus back to Tacoma. I did not grieve her passing. I kept it all bottled up inside me and went on with my life as though nothing had happened. I went through the motions of living life.

I worked, went to meetings, went to church, took care of my husband, worked the steps, and began doing service work for AA. I lived my life according to what my husband thought it should be. He would often tell me that according to the Bible, it was my job to be subservient to him; I did not read the Bible then because I believed I was too stupid to understand it. My husband had become my God, my Higher Power. He was in complete control of my life. He told me when and where to work and the meetings I was to attend. He told me what to talk to my sponsor and what I could not say to her. I was miserable; when I was a little over a year sober, I finally started working the steps of AA.

The first step refers to being powerless over alcohol and life being unmanageable; that was true for me. The second and third steps are about being restored to sanity and putting my life in God's hands. I had a hard time doing that because I believed God didn't want me. The fourth and fifth steps involve telling every deep dark secret to another person. The sixth and seventh steps show us how certain personality traits caused us to behave the way we did and find ourselves in uncharacteristic situations. Steps 8 and 9 are where we go back to all the people we have harmed during our drinking and drinking career and make restitution wherever necessary. The last three steps are often get called the maintenance steps.

In those early days, praying was difficult as I did not know how, nor did I know whether or not anyone heard or cared. They call for us to take a review of the day, make amends where needed, pray and meditate, so that we can close our eyes to sleep with a clear conscience, which gives us the ability to do the work only we can do, help another addict. The Lord's Prayer, the Serenity Prayer, and the Third Step Prayer were what I learned. I needed to have a relationship with God; now, that was a new concept.

In my years in church, I had never heard of anyone having a relationship with God. During this time, I developed a passing relationship with God, who I did not understand in the least, and at that time, the Bible made little or no sense to me. Unfortunately, I stayed so busy that I drove myself to a breakdown. My sponsor suggested I get outside help, and I did. While I was in therapy, I finally confronted all the demons in my life that had haunted me for the past thirty years. At the same time, I got diagnosed with PTSD due to the trauma in my younger years. Did that make them all go away? No, though it took away a good deal of their power over me and gave me the courage to open up and stand up for myself.

It wasn't long before I realized that I was in an abusive, toxic relationship and needed to find a way out again. Our marriage was in trouble, and he suggested marriage counseling at church. I agreed. I found out later that he had been talking to the counselor at the church for some time. During the first session, the counselor asked if I kept a journal; when I said I did, he said I needed to bring it to the next session. There was no next session. My journal is mine, and no one reads that; it is between God and me. I only share what I write in my journal when something comes up that I cannot reconcile in one sitting; anything that carries over to the next day is grounds for calling my sponsor to help me get a different perspective on the situation. I may be a loner, yet I recognize the need to keep critical people close. I could not stay sober by myself; I needed God's help.

We were fighting all the time, and he was becoming increasingly violent. He would punch the wall to keep from hitting me, yet I somehow knew one day that would change. He was a truck driver and was away during the week, so I started planning my escape. I found a place to live, had my car and a job, and filed separately when it came time to do our taxes. I had people from the group go in and repair the damage he had caused, punching holes in the walls. Finally, he came off the road to an empty house and divorce papers. It may sound like the coward's way out, but it was the only way I knew I could get away and stay gone; it was 1994. Shortly after the divorce, I sought the assistance of a financial counselor. Up until then, I did not know how to pay bills, balance a checkbook, and had no idea how to create a budget. As a result, I was always dependent on my husband to take care of the money.

My oldest daughter moved in with me in 1992; she was in her first year of high school. So after the divorce, I went to meetings, quit going to church, became more involved in service work for AA, and tried to learn how to be a single parent to a teenager and did not know how to do that sober. So I became a helicopter parent. I got involved in all of her friendships; I had to know where she was and what she was doing. I was smothering her; I parented out of guilt for all the years I had missed in her life.

Once again, my relationship with God changed, and I realized that Good Orderly Direction was as close as I could get. So I decided to explore the whole relationship-with-God idea. I wanted to know more, and I wanted to know how to have such a thing if it were possible. So I started reading everything I could get my hands on about religion, spirituality, and anything to do with God. Now I was on a quest, and I had no clue where that would take me or how long.

In the spring of 1995, I enrolled in a class that would help prepare me for college. The course got designed for people in early recovery, and there were tests, exercises to work through, and homework. During one of the exercises, the assignment was to write about an outstanding experience from childhood. I couldn't do it, and I could not come up with a single thing from my childhood that was good or happy. I ran from the room in tears, devastated that I would be exposed as an awful person again. Finally, my instructor came and talked to me, and I was able to find one thing; even though it wasn't a happy experience, it wasn't an abusive one. Fortunately since then, I have found some experiences that were not genuinely awful, and they have helped me find a balance to the pain.

I started out wanting to become a child psychologist. I wanted to help children who were like me, and nothing is more interesting to me than the human mind. I got perfect grades in both psychology and English. Although my test scores said I would be a writer or an English teacher, I had no desire to teach, and being a writer was out of the question. I believed I had no creativity or imagination. I was in my second semester when, in August 1996, my mother decided she wanted to be closer to me and moved to Washington from Massachusetts.

I failed a math class, the end of my college education. I fell into a deep depression, isolation, and hopelessness. Finally, my doctor diagnosed me with depression and gave me medication. She gave me Zoloft for depression and amitriptyline for sleep. After several months of taking medicine, the doctor found that antidepressant and antianxiety drugs have the opposite effect on me. So I stopped taking the medication with prayer and meditation and got involved in service work. And my mother and my youngest brother moved in with my daughter and me. My mother agreed as she and my brother traveled across the country to live with me that she wanted to get sober, and I took her to her first meeting. We lived in a two-bedroom townhouse for the first six months until they found an apartment.

As part of my service work, I was also on the treatment and institutions committee. I was going to meetings at MacNeill Island Correctional Facility. One of the men had a substantial amount of sobriety, and we started talking on the phone a few times a week. I had started a relationship with him. Eventually when my mother was about six months sober, she and my brother found an apartment.

My daughter moved into her place out of high school, and I got a one-bedroom apartment.

Although I would like to say that I settled into peaceful quiet life, I did not. I was *dating* someone in prison. He called nearly every day, and I had to be there to take his calls. I was getting tired of being alone, and he was starting to get controlling. He would tell me when to visit him, when to go to meetings, whom I could associate with, and how to dress and behave. However, a man at AA started talking to me, and I decided to go to dinner and a movie with him. He took me to his house saying we would watch a film there. He raped me during the movie and then took me home. That night I called a friend and my sponsor, who took me to the hospital and called the police. I was five years sober, and I was ready to give up.

I started to think that my dad was right. I was stupid, ugly, and unlovable, and no one would ever really want me. So once again, I withdrew, only going to meetings and work. Finally, one day, I decided to go for a drive to clear my head and was gone for the whole day. I came home to seventy angry messages, so after work the next day, I went to the prison in my work uniform and broke up with him. Now, my life got very quiet; I would spend hours sitting at home alone, listening to smooth jazz, writing, or sitting in the dark. I still went to work and meetings but nothing else. I did not want to socialize; I didn't want to go anywhere or do anything. I lived like this for a couple of years, and I was complacent.

I was working at Pizza Hut at the time as a shift manager. Then I started to tire of restaurant work and looked for something different. Toward the end of 1999, I found a job at an auto parts company as a delivery driver. Unfortunately, the owner of my apartment complex sold the property, and I had to move. I found an apartment in Lakewood where my mother and her new husband were the managers. In 2000, the man in prison got out and occasionally showed up at my home group.

One day in early 2000, I was at a meeting, and a man came up to me and asked me out, and I told him no. Then a few days later, he came to me and said, "You will go out with me."

I laughed at him and again turned him down. Eventually, I did agree to go out to coffee with him. Then my car broke down, and he offered to give me a ride home. I consented, and he moved in with me that night. I lived in a one-bedroom apartment at the time. He had no interest in a sexual relationship, merely a place to stay rent-free. Most of the time, I would ask him for sex, and he refused.

Then in November 2000, we had been at the hall all day for a Thanksgiving potluck on Thanksgiving. When we got home, he got mad at me because I did want to cook dinner. He pushed me up against the wall and acted as if he would hit me. I called my mother and her husband, and they came and made him leave. Several days later, he apologized, so I let him come back. This time, my apartment got broken into, and nothing went missing, but things would get moved around. Then one day, the top of my car was cut open, I had a convertible, and my car got ransacked. My daughter would move back in because her husband joined the Navy and was away at basic training. Things went well when my daughter lived with us.

A few weeks after she moved out in the fall of 2001, I told him that if he intended to continue living with me, he would have to start helping out financially. Again he got angry, and he threw his dinner plate at me, pushed me down, and punched me. I got away from him and called the police; he hung the phone up when he realized I was calling the police. I was able to tell the operator that my boyfriend had hit me. Within minutes, there were five police cars in our parking lot, one car from every police agency in the area. When they arrested him, he said I had hit him. They wanted to see the mark, but there wasn't one, and they took him to jail. The police took a report, took some pictures, and instructed me to obtain a restraining order and not take him back as abusers get worse, never better. The next day at my home group meeting, when people asked about my face and shoulder bruises, I told them what had happened.

Some people were angry that I had a restraining order against a fellow AA member. They said I could not do that as it would interfere with his recovery. So I left and did not go to a meeting for nearly ten years. A couple of days later, he returned, and I had to call the police again; he got arrested again. A few months later, I was able to move to a trailer the next town over. I got a different car. One day I got a phone call at work from someone I didn't know, and since I was a driver, I was rarely in the office. So one day, I got off early and decided to call the number he left. It was the boyfriend using a fake name; he said he wanted me to drop the restraining order and tell people that I had made a mistake, that he had never hit me. He was calling from a business, so I called back and asked to speak to the manager. I told the manager what had happened and offered to bring him a copy of the police report and a restraining order.

When I moved out of the apartment to the trailer, a neighbor I had become friendly with asked me for my phone number. He began calling, and we would talk on the phone occasionally. He asked me to spend New Year's Eve 2001 with him, and I did. We spent a lot of time together for the next year, talking and building a solid friendship/relationship. Then suddenly at the end of the year, it ended. I never did know why, although we are friends to this day.

Then in 2002, I flew to Kentucky for my youngest daughter's wedding, where I ran into my first husband. He asked why I never went back home after our divorce; I told him I didn't have a home to go back to and couldn't afford to leave Alaska at the time. He then said that the air force would have paid for me to go home; I never knew that before.

In 2004, I was forty-four years old, fourteen years sober, and a grandmother. My youngest had adopted her niece, who was six months old, and then gave birth to her first son a few months later. I took a good long look at my life and realized that I had no reason to stay in Washington. I wanted to be a good grandmother, and I couldn't do that from three thousand miles away. Hence, I packed what I could, got rid of everything else, loaded my animals into my car, and drove to Kentucky. At the time, I had two cats and two Chinese Shar-Peis. Early in recovery, my sponsor told me that if I could keep a pet or a plant alive for a year, I would be ready for a relationship. So I filled my house with plants and animals, though I was still not prepared for a relationship.

Once in Kentucky, I lived with my daughter, son-in-law, and two toddlers. My youngest daughter and I did not have much of a relationship at that time; I was the mom who had abandoned her, so she thought. Many years later, she would learn the truth of how she came to live with her dad and not me. I refused to tell her because I did not want to interfere with her relationship with her dad. Things went pretty shaky at first. I took care of the kids, kept the house clean, and cooked dinner. I did not venture out very far; sometimes I would walk around the neighborhood with the children; otherwise, I stayed home. I wanted a relationship with my daughter, so I tried to help her out as much as possible.

Shortly after in July, my son-in-law's stepdad, a widower, came over one evening. He brought his seven-year-old granddaughter from his previous marriage that he was raising. We sat and visited for several hours, and he asked if I would mind watching his granddaughter for him. So over the next month and a half, I watched her and got to know him better. Unfortunately, he had a girlfriend, so I did not give him much thought.

My daughter and her husband fought quite a bit, and I would go into my room and try to ignore it. Finally one night around Thanksgiving, they got into a pretty bad fight, and I began to think that maybe I had made a mistake in moving there, but I was stuck. I did not have a job; the car I had driven across the country got repossessed, and I had nowhere to go.

I began thinking that maybe I would get a job working nights to still take care of the children or work during the day while they were in school. I was planning another escape, but where would I go. I didn't want to go back to Washington; I had no one there. I had family in Michigan though I doubted they would take me in. I had my mother and brothers who had moved back to Massachusetts, and I did not want to move back to Massachusetts. So I stayed in Kentucky and tried to make the best of the situation. I tried going to a couple of meetings, but it was too inconvenient since I had no car. Finally it reached a point where I would fix dinner, and as soon as the children were in bed, I went to my room.

Loneliness, poor decisions, and depression began to set in, and I isolated more each day. Since I wasn't going to meetings, I did not have a support system. I was alone again. I turned to God and thought again about trying to develop a relationship with Him. Going to church was out of the question, but I could go to the library; I had a Bible and a Big Book and began reading both. I journaled more as I had no one to talk to, so I started talking directly to God. I started each day with a "Dear God" letter. Eventually around eleven o'clock at night in early December, my son-in-law's stepdad called me and asked if I wanted to go to dinner. Unfortunately, he was drunk, and I had already eaten. So to get out of the house, I went to a restaurant with him, where I ordered a piece of pie and made him get a burger and coffee; that was December 9, 2005. We sat there, ate, and talked until nearly sunrise. Over the next few weeks, we spoke on the phone almost every day. And then a huge fight broke out between my daughter and her husband while I was putting the children down for bed.

My little three-year-old granddaughter whispered, "Make them stop, Grandma." What could I do? I went out and tried to ask them to stop. My daughter turned on me and told me to get out of the house, and I left. My daughter called me when I was a couple of blocks away and apologized; she tried to convince me to return. There was no way I was walking back into that house anytime soon. I had enough of being tormented in my life and did not desire to take it from my child. It was supposed to be a fresh start, a new beginning for me; it wasn't going the way I thought.

While my daughter was on the phone with me, her husband called his stepdad and told him I was walking down the road toward his house. I didn't know exactly how to get there, but I had a general idea and thought I could find his truck and see where the place was. He woke up his granddaughter, and they came to find me and took me back to their house. The next day we decided that I should move there with them. He bought me a car for Christmas and asked me to marry him three weeks later.

We were married five months later in May 2006. I had been working as a delivery driver for an auto parts store at the time, and he asked me to quit. He wanted me to stay home and take care of our granddaughter and the other three grandkids. It was a tough decision for me; I had worked since I was sixteen and supported myself since my divorce in 1994, although not very well. I did not know how to trust anyone that much to take care of me financially. I had to learn how to rely on someone, something I had struggled to overcome many years before. It was a whole new learning experience for me.

We visited several of the caves under Kentucky for our honeymoon. Like me, he had been married three times before and had never had a honeymoon. He decided he wanted to explore the caves because it was one of those things he had always wanted to do and never had the opportunity previously. He taught me how to fish, and we did a little sightseeing and camping near Cumberland Dam. Life was pretty rocky at first. He was used to being single, and so was I, and his granddaughter was in charge of the house; I was an intruder. Sometimes, he would come home from work, work in the garden, get drunk, and sleep. Some nights he wouldn't come home from work until well after seven or eight in the evening, drunk. I started to feel like a live-in babysitter and maid. My granddaughter felt the same way, and she treated me as such.

Since I was not her grandmother, she thought she did not have to listen to me and rarely did. Finally one day he came home from work, and she went to him and told him that I was mean to her and wanted me to leave. I told him what she had done that day, and he told me to work it out; he would not be a referee.

At the time, my granddaughter had infrequent rules to follow, and I decided it was time she had a few. She did not have a routine respite, rarely bathed, and her room was disgusting. I set her a regular bedtime, told her she was to take a bath at least on school nights, and she had to clean her room. She did not like it, but she followed them because he told her she had to listen to me. I told her that she had a week to clean her room or I was going to, and she would not like it. She decided to test me and did nothing. So after a week passed, I took a garbage bag and went into her room and cleaned it. I threw away nearly everything on the floor, filling the garbage bag. When she got home from school, she was in a rage; how dare I throw away her things. She went to my husband and was even angrier when he told her I warned her. We rarely had to ask her to clean her room more than once after that.

She decided to change tactics; if he wouldn't make me leave, then she would; she came to me one day and said that he had several other girlfriends, and that was why he didn't come home. I didn't know what to believe; I was in another relationship with someone I barely knew. I talked to him about it later, and he denied it. He did become more attentive to me and began including me when he went places, even if he thought I wouldn't be interested. Then a few years later, I woke up one morning and opened the computer to check my email and Facebook accounts. I found that he had left his Facebook messenger open. The night before, he talked to an old girlfriend on the computer. I felt rejected; here I was lying in bed waiting for him, and he was telling another woman he loved her. That afternoon when he came home from work, I confronted him. I simply asked if I needed to leave. After that, he began to make an effort to be home more, and I took charge of caring for our granddaughter.

In time we settled into a comfortable existence. We would often go fishing on the weekends; I was not very good at it, so I would bring a book and relax while my husband fished. We went camping near a creek in Bardstown every July 4 weekend. I truly enjoyed it. We would go fishing, relax, and talk for two or three days away from the noise of the fireworks. Life was tranquil, and I became content. Or so I thought; what I was, was complacent. I wasn't happy, but I wasn't unhappy either. I still took care of my other grandchildren, and now there were three.

My daughter and her husband divorced, and she went back to school. We supported her as much as we could. Then on July 4, 2012, our annual camping trip was rained out; I was devastated. I sat on the patio and cried most of the day, watching the rain and wishing for a drink, questioning, "Is this why I got sober? Is this my life?" I thought if I just got drunk, I would not have to feel any of this pain. That thinking let me know I was in real trouble, and I decided I needed to get back to AA and fast.

For a recovering alcoholic, that kind of thinking is borderline suicidal thinking since, for most of us, to drink is to die. Somehow I knew that if I started drinking again, I would not stop, and I may not make it back to recovery. I was nearly twenty-three years sober at the time. It had been ten years since I had set foot in an AA meeting, and I was as scared as I had been all those years before. I started going to a Big Book study on Sunday mornings; most of the people there were from a local treatment center. I needed to get a sponsor and did not know any women when someone suggested I go to a women's meeting the following Monday night. I took care of the kids before and after school and in the summer.

We went on adventures, water parks, museums, and the zoo (my favorite). Sometimes we would just hang out in the backyard or walk around the neighborhood. We also helped in the garden; my husband planted vegetables every year, giving him a little relaxation when he came home from work. Also that year, my oldest daughter left her husband and moved to Kentucky. She stayed with us for a while. Then after finding a job and an apartment, she eventually remarried. Her arrival here also meant a rekindled relationship between her and her sister. One day, I spent the day with my youngest daughter, and she was dropping me off when she asked for a favor. I didn't want to do it, but I still felt like I needed to make amends for her feeling abandoned. She knew I wanted to say no, yet I didn't. Before I got out of the car, she looked at me and told me that it was okay for me to say no and that she forgave me. Those were the most incredible words I had ever heard, and I shed tears of gratitude. I found out later that her sister had told her about their dad declaring me legally unfit and taking custody of them away from me.

He would take a weekend and go hunting with his brother in the fall. That was pretty much our life until one evening when I asked if I could learn how to hunt. I was no stranger to guns; I had been around them most of my life. My husband was thrilled, so I got to go on the annual weekend hunting trip, and the first year, I got my first buck. Talk about elated! It made the whole trip worthwhile. We got up around three in the morning and drove an hour out to the farm where we hunted. Then we walked in the dark across an open field to the tree stand. I climbed up in the tree and waited until daylight.

As I sat there listening and praying, I felt excitement and anxiety. Could I do this? Getting a deer would mean meat in the freezer and substantial savings on our grocery bill. Then a little after sunrise, this deer wandered right up to the tree where I sat. We got him home, and my husband taught me how to process the deer and get it in the freezer. It was a great source of pride for me to know that I could provide meat for my family.

In the years since that time, we found a new hunting place; we would go the day before and stay in a camp trailer with his brother. We would build a fire and talk while they drank. Then the following day, opening day, we would get up before daylight and make our way up into the woods. Hunting season is in late October, so it's usually pretty cold, and before dawn, it's the hardest. I walked in the woods in the dark to a spot I chose the day before and then hunkered down to wait. These predawn hours are my favorite; I pray and listen.

On frigid mornings, sitting quietly, every sound is amplified; a frozen leaf falling from a tree can sound like a squirrel scampering around. I've heard people say that deer are exceptionally quiet moving through the forest; however, you can listen to them if you know what to listen for; you can listen to them. If they are running, it sounds like a stampede; if they are walking and grazing, they move very slowly and, therefore, very quietly. I have been sitting waiting for them to appear more than once, and the next thing I know, there's one only a few feet away.

By this time, all the grandkids were in school. So my husband and I talked it over and decided it was time for me to go back to college and finish my degree, changing it once again to chemical dependency for adolescents. So the following fall, 2016, I enrolled in college; at the same time, my daughter found out she was pregnant with baby number 3. She had remarried sometime before, and they wanted a child. In the spring of 2017, I had another new grandson. I was in college, online, full-time, and taking care of an infant. It was a bit of a struggle, but I made it work; my husband helped when he could. I had to take statistics during the second year, and I panicked. I even called my advisor to try and find a different class.

My husband was very supportive, and my advisor said all I needed to pass the course was a sixty percent. I made it through with a seventy-five. I wanted to graduate, and I was getting to the end of my classes. In January 2019, I had seven courses left to take, and my husband decided to retire. I took two lessons and was down to five. Shortly after he retired, he fell into a depression for nearly four months. These bouts of depression were not new for him, and he usually pulled himself out of them pretty quickly, so I did not push him. However, I would encourage him to get up and spend time with the kids or me. I was going to the gym at the time and started taking a water aerobics class and wanted him to come with me.

After about four or five months, he finally agreed, he didn't want to join my group, but he would walk the treadmill and work out on the weights. I decided to take one course in the summer since my husband was retired, and we could spend more time together. I still had the baby during the day, so we only did things on the weekend. Eventually he began working part-time with his brother and going fishing with a friend he had known since childhood. Before he retired, he had started frequenting a local bar. Sometimes he would be gone for an hour or so, and other times, I would call him, and if he answered, I would tell him his dinner was in the microwave, and I was going to bed. Eventually he also started walking with me occasionally and going to the gym.

For some reason, putting in a garden that year seemed more than he was willing to do, but I didn't question it then. One evening in September, after the kids had left, we walked around the neighborhood; while talking, he apologized for not putting in a garden. I told him there was always next year, and he said, "If I'm still here." I questioned him, but he said it was just a comment, and I chose to ignore it.

In November 2019, we were getting ready for our annual hunting trip. We got into probably the most powerful argument of our marriage over something so trivial that it would not have been an issue under normal circumstances. The rules of our entire thirteen-year marriage were that we always said "I love you" before we left or before we went to sleep. And we never went to sleep angry. That night was no exception. He and his brother left for the camp early the following day, which I would follow later in the day.

As I was getting ready for the day, he told me that maybe it would be better if I waited until first thing in the morning as he didn't want me driving in the dark. He knew I enjoyed having the house to myself and God, so I agreed to stay home. My relationship with God had grown over time, yet I still wasn't sure what I believed. I prayed every day and would talk to Him every day, but I still had doubts about whether or not He wanted anything to do with me. So I stayed home and enjoyed some quality quiet time. At six-thirty that evening, he called. He was getting pretty drunk, but we had a good conversation. "I love you, and see you in the morning." These were to be the last words we said to each other. My brother-in-law called and told me my husband had collapsed and got taken to the hospital at ten-thirty.

I jumped up and headed out the door when it occurred to me I needed to let my daughter know what was going on. So I called her and told her that I would call her when I had more information. That was not going to work; she insisted on coming with me and was already on her way. God was in that situation, and I knew because I started praying before getting off the phone with my brother-in-law. We were halfway to the hospital when my phone rang; it was the coroner. He told me not to go to the hospital as my husband was not there. He had been pronounced dead at the camp. So while my daughter drove for the next half hour, I made phone calls to family and friends to let them know what had happened. I talked to the coroner, answered all his questions, and we came home.

I sent my family home as I needed some time to myself. I barely moved off the couch for the whole day. The next day was Sunday, and I had arrangements to make and people to call, but first, I needed my other family, and I went to the eight-forty-five Sunday meeting. Only by God's grace was I able to make it through that next month. Everything felt surreal; I was in a nightmare that would not end; I was numb. And then I started running, a behavior I had long since given up; I ran to meetings, events, and anywhere that was not home and did not remind me of my husband. I barely grieved, nor did I feel. I did, however, attend a grief support group for a while, though I felt out of place, and after six weeks, I quit going.

I celebrated my thirtieth sobriety anniversary, and two months later, my sixtieth birthday was in a fog. And then on March 1, 2020,

I got a phone call at six in the morning from my husband's half-brother; his youngest son had died in the night. Great. Someone I could help and not think about myself or my pain. So back on the shelf it went. And then COVID hit. Lockdown, isolation, I still found a way to run; I began walking up to six miles a day so that I could sleep a few hours a night. Alcoholics Anonymous started having meetings online so people could stay connected, but that did not work for me; I needed people. Then the club where I went to meetings got classified as an essential business, and we were able to have in-person meetings within the recommended guidelines set forth by the CDC. At the fourth of July celebration, which, although subdued per restrictions, I ran into a lady I had seen at a few meetings. We sat together most of the day, and as things progressed, we found we had quite a lot in common, and much of our lives paralleled. We have since become very close friends.

I did grieve some then, although mostly I prayed. I screamed mostly, begging God to let me die, to show me how to cope with the pain. However it felt like God wasn't listening.

We decided in August 2019 that my brothers and my mother would move to Kentucky the following year. My mother is wheelchair-bound, and my brothers had been taking care of her and needed help. So I agreed that the youngest would come down in August, and I would travel to Massachusetts and bring my other brother and mother down. I still had not allowed myself more than a few hours to grieve. It was as though I did not know how; I knew he was with God, and he was happy. He died doing the things he loved and with people who loved him. Somehow I had to find a way to move on with my life, but I was still in running mode. I was rearranging my entire world. Different meetings, different people, different places, constantly moving.

So in August 2020, my brother moved in, and I did everything to help him find a job and an apartment. He found a job pretty quickly but was dragging his feet about finding an apartment. So a month and a half later, I went to Massachusetts and brought my mother and brother down. That was the first time I had been back to Massachusetts since my grandmother passed away in 1991. I had a feeling I would not be going back there again, so there were some things I wanted to take care of for my sanity. I needed to go to the beach; I needed to go to the places that still haunted my nightmares. I had to make peace with myself around this place. So after driving for over eighteen hours, I went to the beach, to the exact spot I got raped all those years ago. All I saw was the beach, the waves crashing against the shore, the smell of the sea air, the cry of the seagulls in the early morning light, and the sound of traffic on the street behind me. There was no fear, no pain, no anxiety, only the beach that I had always turned to for comfort as a child. I sat there, and I prayed and thanked God for peace.

They stayed in a hotel for two weeks and then decided they wanted to go to Tennessee with my uncle for a while to give Michael a chance to get them a place to live. It had been many years since I had seen my uncle; I barely knew my aunt and cousins and had only met one of their nine children thirty years before. But I will never forget the moment I saw that young man; he walked up the steps and gave me the biggest hug I had received in a very long time. Before returning to Kentucky, I spent some time with my cousin and his wife.

My granddaughter and I ventured into Nashville before heading back home. I had always wanted to see the Grand Ole Opry, and I did. Though I was getting there, I had not come to terms with my grief. I was beginning to come to terms with my life in general, and I started making an effort to move forward with my life.

In October 2020, I met someone I had seen many times over the past four years but never got the opportunity to meet. A neighbor, who had lived down the street, we would say hello but never really spoke.

In early November, I went back to my cousin's house to get reacquainted with a boy I had not seen since thirteen in 1991. I wanted to know the man he had become. My relationship with God became more prominent, deeper, and meaningful than before during that weekend. COVID was winding down a bit; some of the restrictions were easing up, and people were getting out again. My daughter and her family and I went to Tennessee for Thanksgiving and got to know the rest of the family; it was a spectacular weekend. During that weekend, my family and I decided to put my mother in a nursing home. She uses a wheelchair, and moving her was unsafe for her or the person lifting her. So when I came back home, I made the arrangements for my mother's care. Both brothers were living with me, and I felt very crowded. Birthdays, holidays, and anniversaries came with excitement and enthusiasm, though not the same attitude. A void from losing my husband and COVID seemed to fill every happy occasion.

In April 2021, I started slowing down, settling back into a routine, meetings, and taking care of my grandson and home. Then I was sitting at a light one day, and my neighbor came up next to me. I rolled down my window, and he asked me if I was married; it was the first time I had to say out loud, "I am a widow." A few days later, we exchanged phone numbers. After that, he and I started walking, talking, hanging out, and getting to know each other. He's a Christian, which helped me ask some questions I had never been able to ask before and learn some things I had never considered before about myself. Life was beginning to calm down.

One night at a meeting, a woman I had known for many years came to me and asked how I coped with losing my husband. Her husband was nearing the end of his life. She did not know what to do or how she would manage. Her situation was different from mine, yet the future would be the same; she would be a widow. I told her to hold on to the people she loved and let them help her, something I did not do. As it turned out, shortly after her husband died, she also passed away. That's when I followed my advice; I held onto the people in my life and let them be there for me even though it was a struggle to ask for help. Unfortunately I had very few people left by this time as my running had driven the rest away.

I walked again, went to meetings, participated in social events, and spent time with my family. Finally, my brothers found an apartment, and I got my house back.

Then in June 2021, my cousin from Tennessee was killed. I was going through another inventory with my sponsor when I got the news. I had done several reviews over the past two years, trying to make my life make sense. I drove down to Tennessee for the funeral and spent some time with the family. After the service, I suddenly felt an urgency to go home. God was telling me it was time to leave. I got in my car, and I had the strangest feeling I have ever had; it was as if someone was in the car with me. I could feel a presence in the vehicle. This presence stayed with me all the way home. Something in me changed on that drive home, something profound that I could not put my finger on; I only knew I was different inside somehow. I was still going to a few meetings outside of my home group, walking occasionally, and spending time with friends. Then one night, I was on my way to a meeting; my daughter called and said her husband had COVID.

Something inside me broke; I was angry; I gave up. I began making a plan; when I got home, I was going to take the entire prescription of trazodone I had refilled that day. I drove, cried, prayed, and decided I just wanted to go to sleep and not wake up. I did not think about anyone else, only that I quit. I was done with death, COVID, losing friends, isolation, and loneliness. When I made it home, that still small voice told me to call the lady across the street and give her the medication. I did. I called no one else.

One lady called me and talked to me for a few minutes, and it helped me calm down. The next call I got made everything so much worse. A lady I knew called, and when I told her what happened, she began yelling at me. I was immediately taken back to when I was a child. She scolded me for mistreating and being selfish to my family and the people who cared about me. By the time I got off the phone with her, I felt worse than before. I sat on my front porch and cried and prayed until I couldn't cry anymore, I thought. I went to bed, and as I lay there trying to sleep, my mind got flooded with everything from the last two years. I finally sat up in my bed and screamed and cried and got angry.

When I eventually fell asleep out of sheer exhaustion, I was able to sleep for about three or four hours. God has put some highly intuitive people in my life, and I cannot be grateful enough for them. First my best friend called and asked what was going on; I was pretty ashamed and could not tell him the truth. Then my sponsor called, and I told her everything, and we came up with a plan of action. Even though I got quarantined, there were still things I could do. First I called my doctor, and then when my best friend called back, I told him the whole truth. He stayed on the phone with me for three days, talking to me and encouraging me. When we weren't on the phone, we were texting. Finally he texted me something that I clung to, "I will not be defeated," in capital letters.

When my doctor called later, she changed my medication, diagnosed me with major depressive disorder, and recommended I seek therapy. I stayed home for two weeks. During that time, I realized I needed to make some significant changes in my life; I could no longer live the way I had been living, or I was going to die. One night I was at my best friend's house and told him I was going back to church. The following Sunday, I looked up church services in the directory and found one with a service at eight-thirty in the morning. I showed up there at around eight-fifteen. There was not a single car in the parking lot. So I waited; there was still no one there by eight-thirty. Finally, I got on Google and looked for the next nearest service with the next closest church. I was a mile away, and the service started at nine. I walked in and was greeted at the door, shown to my seat, and when I sat down, I looked up at the wall, and in great big letters, it said, "You belong here."

I started to cry, and within minutes, a lady came up to me and talked to me. It wasn't until the worship team came out that I realized God led me to a multi-racial Christian church. God always knows what he's doing even when it makes no sense to us. He puts us right where He needs us when He needs us there. Then during the sermon, the pastor said something that I will never forget. "We will not be defeated." All at once, my life began to change. I had finally found what I had been missing in church for my entire life—love, understanding, and hope. I walked out of there feeling like I was walking on a cloud. Finally I looked up and told God, "That's what church is supposed to feel like." The next day, I rewatched both sermons from the day before, and then I went to the website, joined the church, and rededicated my life to Christ.

A few weeks later, I found a therapist; she was terrific. She knew about people in recovery and grief. She had me do some reflection work on myself. Some things I discovered during those few sessions. My husband may have known he was going to die. He commented about not being here to plant a garden the following year, but then I realized there were other comments. Our granddaughter had moved out right after she graduated, and one day, my husband said he had fulfilled his promise to do his job. He had promised her grandmother that he would keep and raise her.

Unfortunately after about four sessions, she needed to make some changes and had to leave. So God found a new therapist for me, a Christian woman. She is fantastic. In January 2022, I went on a retreat with some women from the church. Though I almost did not get to go, one Sunday after church, I talked to a couple of ladies about the retreat, and they asked if I was going. I said I couldn't afford it. They told me they would pay for it if I wanted to go. All I can say is that it was an incredible life-changing experience.

Going back to church was the best decision I ever made. Was this where I intended my life to go? Nope, not even close. Yet here I am. Right where God wanted me to be. The church I belong to is full of the most loving, kind, compassionate, and beautiful group of people I have ever met. They don't see me as odd or strange; they see me as a whole person. Since then, everything has changed. I still struggle with loneliness and depression, yet I have people I can rely on who help bring me back up. Life continues to change because I am willing to embrace the changes as they happen. I am learning new things, and life is vastly different from a year ago, a month ago, and yesterday.

The Light Is On

My life is vastly different today than at the beginning of this journey. Where I came from is lightyears away from where I am now, and it is a fantastic blessing to wake up every day and know that I am a loved, wanted, gifted child of God. Today while I am still a loner. I have a core group of people who have helped, encouraged, loved, and supported me that God placed in my life when I needed them most. These five people are the only ones who know and see me, and they helped me learn how to love and accept myself. They taught me to understand that I am stronger than I think I am and helped me to keep moving forward no matter what. As a result, today, I can take on challenges I never thought I could before.

Today, I know who I am, and I am aware of my life's impact on those around me. There are a few things I try to keep in the forefront of my mind: I may be the only Big Book/Bible some people ever read; everything happens for a reason, and change is inevitable, so embrace it and always remain teachable. I am a far cry from perfect, and that's okay today. I have a God who loves and forgives me. There have been many times when I wanted to quit, to give up, but God always rescued me in one way or another. I am far from perfect. I am not the *goody two-shoes* I was called in school.

Today I have a wonderful relationship with my children and grandchildren, who have helped, loved, supported, and stood by me through the most difficult and darkest times of my life. My brothers also live nearby and help me out as often as they can. My mother is in a nursing home as she is wheelchair-bound. Today we are a family.

I have wanted my bedroom painted for nearly seventeen years as it looked awful like they didn't paint it since they built the house in 1961. Finally one Sunday morning at breakfast with my daughter, I told her I would give up the idea of painting my room because I couldn't afford it. A man at another table asked if I wanted his phone number as he remodeled houses for a living. A few weeks later, he came over and gave me an estimate, and then he never called back. I decided I would do it myself, even though I had never done anything like that before and did not know what I was doing or how to do it. I am learning; not only did I do my room, but also now the second bedroom is painted. The next project is the kitchen and dining room. I get to learn how to remove wallpaper and replace the backsplash.

I have opened my home to people in transition, something I would never have done before. But as I would tell everyone, roommates are a terrible idea since I don't play well with others.

I spend many hours by myself, reading and working on the house; today I enjoy my own company and relish the quiet of simply listening to nature. Thunderstorms, tree frogs, and the whip-poor-will song are the most comforting sounds.

The next thing I want to learn is car maintenance. I have always paid someone else to work on my cars, and I think I can do it myself.

I still want to do many things with my life, and today I know that I can.